OVERCOMING BUSYNESS

OVERCOMING BUSYNESS

RESTING IN GOD DURING LIFE'S DEMANDS AND RESPONSIBILITIES

A 10-LESSON BIBLE STUDY

DAVID RUSTAD

Table of Contents

Introduction

I t often feels like the pace of life is speeding up. More to-dos. More activities. More options. More shiny objects calling for our attention. Too often, this breathless commotion simply leads to … more busyness!

Busyness is not unique to people in the 21st century. In fact, busyness has been a common challenge for people of all ages and times.

God has much to say about how we ought to live in the midst of life's demands, responsibilities and opportunities.

This Bible study—*Overcoming Busyness*—is designed to help us better understand busyness from a biblical perspective. Through the lives of Martha, Saul, Moses, David, Haggai and Jesus, we'll examine how God would have us deal with busyness and find our rest in him.

At times, this may mean:
- Re-focusing our priorities
- Surrendering our desires
- Rejecting our false expectations

- Choosing service over being served

Overcoming Busyness is not a self-help, 10-step program designed to erase the daily responsibilities, pressures and busyness of life. Sorry!

Rather, *Overcoming Busyness* is meant to help us navigate-- through God's strength and wisdom--the many demands pulling on our lives. As we invite him into the whole of our lives, we can be certain that he will guide and direct. He will give us all that we need to endure, prosper and rest.

May you experience God's blessings as you study his word and seek to live as he desires.

Soli Deo Gloria (glory to God alone)!

Lesson 1

Focus on God's To-Dos
(Based on Luke 10:38-42)

Personal study: 15 to 20 minutes
Group discussion: 45 to 50 minutes

I f anyone ever deserved a pat on the back, it was Martha. Jesus--and perhaps his entire disciple crew--were in town and needed a place to stay. "Hey, you can rest here," she offered.

While we can't know Martha's exact preparations, the invitation brought with it a significant amount of work. Perhaps: cleaning the house; planning meals; prepping food; re-arranging the sleeping quarters. ... Whatever it was, her to-do list was likely long, and she started feeling the pressure.

To make matters worse, Martha wasn't receiving the support she expected from her sister, Mary. "Why am I doing all the work alone while Mary is 'goofing off' listening to Jesus," she might have thought. Ever felt like a martyr because of the to-dos on your list?

The resentment began to boil over, so she asked Jesus to prod Mary into action.

1

Jesus' response wasn't what Martha was expecting. He lauded Mary's actions while gently reprimanding Martha. Jesus' point? To-dos are less important than people, and our relationship with him takes priority over everything else.

That isn't to say that Martha's household tasks weren't important; they just weren't MOST important. That's one of the damaging downsides of busyness: "the important" gets swallowed up by "the urgent."

As we begin this study, ask yourself these questions:
• Am I pausing today to recognize that Jesus is seeking me?
• Can I trust God to organize (or reorganize) my to-dos?
• What can I change to be faithful to God yet address my responsibilities?

Now read more what the Bible says about busyness and focusing on God's to-dos.

Read Luke 10:38-42

Q-1. What was Mary's focus during Jesus' visit? What was Martha's focus (Luke 10:38-40a)?

_____

_____

_____

Q-2. What did Martha ask of Jesus (Luke 10:40b)? Was her request reasonable? Why? What do you typically do when you feel others are not helping with the responsibilities you carry?

_____

_____

_____

Focus on God's To-Dos

Note: Martha was "distracted" (i.e., over-occupied or too busy) with all the preparations (literally, "much serving"). Rather than choosing simple means to meet Jesus' needs, Martha had probably opted to go "super elaborate." Martha was so immersed in her vision of elegant hosting that she failed to spend time with the one who was her guest.

Q-3. What surprising reply did Jesus give Martha (Luke 10:41)? Are you more prone to be worried and upset when you're busy? Why?

_____

_____

_____

_____

Q-4. Is it wrong to have to-dos and goals in daily life? If not, what makes the difference between a good to-do and a bad one?

_____

_____

_____

Q-5. Martha appears to be a "Type A" personality. What are the potential upsides and downsides of being "driven?"

_____

_____

_____

_____

Overcoming Busyness

Note: At times, Type A personalities (i.e., those high energy, goal-oriented, do-it-now, take-charge folks) may wish they could be more like "Type B's" (i.e., those relaxed, no-urgency, pause-to-enjoy, adaptable folks). Even a personality transplant, however, cannot erase busyness from our lives. God gifted you with your personality. What matters most is that we give ourselves completely to Christ!

Q-6. What, according to Jesus, is truly needed (Luke 10:42)? What does spending time with Jesus look like today? How do you do this in your life?

_____

_____

_____

_____

Q-7. Are you more like Mary or more like Martha? Why?

_____

_____

_____

_____

Q-8. Why do you think Jesus prioritized spending time with him above Martha's housework? How, if at all, are your current responsibilities crimping your time with Jesus?

_____

_____

_____

_____

Q-9. What did Jesus promise about the time Mary gave to him (Luke 10:42)? How does this apply to you today?

_____

_____

_____

Q-10. How do you balance your daily (important) responsibilities with the most important responsibility of your relationship, i.e., "time," with Jesus? How might you simplify your to-dos to make more time for Jesus and others? Be specific!

_____

_____

_____

_____

Q-11. Record one important biblical principle (i.e., a promise, command, lesson or truth) you learned from God's word and how you intend to apply it to your life this week. Be specific!

_____

_____

_____

Observation: Time with Jesus (e.g., through scripture reading, prayer, meditation) may feel like just one more "to-do." In fact, time together with the one who intimately knows, loves and desires you (i.e., Jesus!) is the best-invested time of all.

Key Reminder: Jesus seeks a relationship with you because he loves you -- even in your busyness!

Lesson 2

Seek God When Under Pressure

(Based on 1 Samuel 10:6-8, 13:1-14)

Personal study: 15 to 20 minutes
Group discussion: 45 to 50 minutes

S aul was the newly anointed King of Israel. It's not a role he sought. In fact, the day he was publicly announced as king by the Prophet Samuel, Saul "hid out" (1 Samuel 10:17-24) to avoid the attention. Still, God had work for Saul to do.

Some time later in Saul's reign, the Philistines, enemies of God's people, began menacing Israel. Saul then had his son, Jonathan, attack a Philistine outpost. The Philistine army gathered in numbers that now dwarfed King Saul's army.

Seek God When Under Pressure

Samuel had earlier instructed Saul to travel to Gilgal and to wait for him there for seven days. He told Saul he would give him further instructions at that time (1 Samuel 10:8).

That sounds simple enough, but in the meantime, King Saul's soldiers were deserting, and the circumstances became dire!

Now King Saul had a decision to make: Take action on his own, or continue to wait for Samuel (God's prophet and messenger). In fact, this was a choice for Saul between relying on his own abilities and wisdom … or relying on God.

Saul opted to act in his own power. In that decision, he forfeited much of the blessing that God had promised him.

Rarely are we confronted with life and death decisions, but we regularly face the choice that Saul did. Under pressure, do we act in our own power … or do we wait for God's direction? Busyness—with all its urgency—tends to push us into taking action in our own power ... without God.

It's important to remember that God's timing is not our timing. God is never late – even when we are under pressure!

Now read more what the Bible says about busyness and seeking God when under pressure.

Read 1 Samuel 10:6-8, 13:1-14

Q-1. What did Samuel instruct Saul to do when he reached Gilgal (1 Samuel 10:6-8)? Is "waiting" difficult for you? Why?

_____

_____

_____

Q-2. What do you typically do when the path forward is unclear or challenging? Cite a specific example, if you can.

_____

_____

_____

Q-3. Did Saul disobey, partially obey or fully obey Samuel's instructions (1 Samuel 13:1-14)? How is your obedience to God affected by busyness and pressure?

_____

_____

_____

_____

Q-4. What was the general attitude of those in King Saul's army (1 Samuel 13:6-8)? Where do you turn when you are "hard pressed" by difficult circumstances or fear?

_____

_____

_____

_____

Note: _Saul was very aware of Samuel's previous instructions related to gathering at Gilgal (1 Samuel 10:8). Rather than waiting for Samuel to make an offering to God, Saul took matters into his own hands._

Q-5. What was wrong with Saul's decision to make an offering to God (1 Samuel 13:9)? What were Saul's motives for doing this?

_____

_____

_____

_____

Note: *Saul likely felt that given his current circumstances--the gathering of a powerful, enemy army--he didn't have time to obey either God's law or God's prophet. On both accounts, he was sadly mistaken!*

Q-6. How did King Saul respond to being "caught" in his disobedience (1 Samuel 13:11-12)? Have you ever made excuses to God for your disobedience? What is the proper thing to do when we fail to obey God?

_____

_____

_____

_____

Q-7. What was the result of King Saul's disobedience (1 Samuel 13:13-14)?

_____

_____

_____

_____

Overcoming Busyness

Note: *King Saul's successor--David--also sinned in God's sight (e.g., committed adultery with Bathsheba; murdered Uriah; failed to address/punish sinful actions of sons; counted his fighting men [contrary to God's command]). And yet ... David was called "a man after God's heart" because he repented and leaned into God for grace and mercy (See Psalm 51:1).*

Q-8. To be clear, "busyness" is not "sinfulness." However, busyness (and pressure) can foster self-reliance that forgets God. Take a moment to honestly survey the stresses, pressures and busyness in your life. Are you facing this busyness in your own strength or in God's? Explain.

_____

_____

_____

_____

Q-9. Record one important biblical principle (i.e., a promise, command, lesson or truth) you learned from God's word and how you intend to apply it to your life this week. Be specific!

_____

_____

_____

_____

Observation: Even in times of pressure, God calls us not to greater self-effort but to greater dependence and trust in him.

Key Reminder: Despite our sin, God loves us. Our relationship with God is "grace based," not "performance based" because of Christ's redeeming work on our behalf.

Lesson 3

Rest in God's Goodness (Worship)
(Based on Genesis 2:2-3, Exodus 20:8-11, Mark 2:23-28)

Personal study: 15 to 20 minutes
Group discussion: 45 to 50 minutes

I remember well when my kindergarten classmates and I rolled out rugs we had brought to school and laid down for 15 minutes of daily rest. ... What a concept!

That may not be the current practice in kindergarten classrooms, but back in the day this rest period allowed me and my squirrelly classmates to recharge and refocus before beginning afresh with the many things we needed to learn in class.

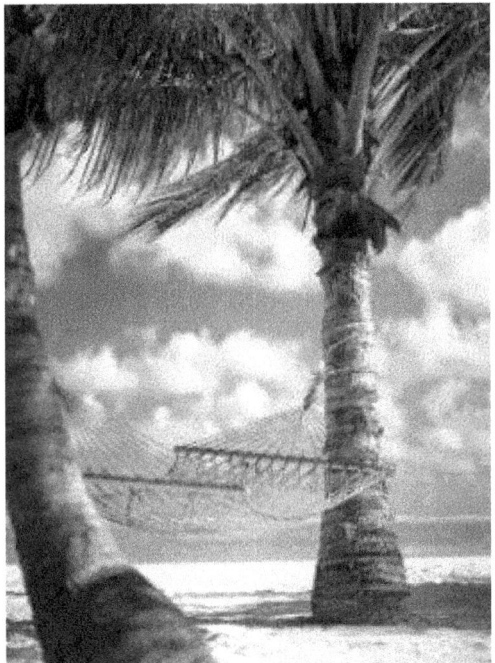

Moses recorded God's command that we take a break from the busy rhythm of life to rest and reflect on God's goodness. God's command to rest was based on God's work in creation (Genesis 2:1-3). This time of rest, the Sabbath, was specifically a time set apart by God for his people.

Today many Christians observe the Sabbath on Sunday. Unfortunately, this "rest" is often riddled with busyness (e.g., shopping, eating out, household errands, football, and more!).

Busyness squeezes our time of rest and distracts us from focusing on the goodness of God. It's a detour that does not serve us well.

As we begin:
• What does the Sabbath really mean for you today?
• How do you truly obey and honor God, both in your work and in your rest?
• How do you trust God with rest when your life is busy?

Now read more what the Bible says about busyness and resting in God's goodness.

Read Genesis 2:2-3; Exodus 20:8-11; Mark 2:23-28

Q-1. What came before God's seventh day of rest (Genesis 2:2-3)? What does God's blessing of this day tell you about **your** need for rest?

_____

_____

_____

_____

Rest in God's Goodness (Worship)

Note: The Hebrew word translated here as "rest" comes from the word "Sabbath." It conveys the idea of ceasing, resting or desisting from exertion ("H7673 - šāḇaṯ - Strong's Hebrew Lexicon (KJV)." Blue Letter Bible. Accessed 25 Mar, 2021. https://www.blueletterbible.org//lang/lexicon/lexicon.cfm?Strongs=H7673&t=KJV).

Q-2. God made the seventh day "holy," that is, set it apart, consecrated it, dedicated it to himself (Genesis 2:3). Are holiness and busyness compatible? Explain.

_____

_____

_____

_____

Q-3. In Exodus 20:8, God again calls his people to keep his day of rest "holy." What does this currently look like in your life?

_____

_____

_____

Q-4. Why does God tell us that those under our influence (e.g., children, servants, animals, visitors) should keep the Sabbath as well (Exodus 20:8-10)? What are the implications for you in your relationship with others?

_____

_____

_____

_____

Overcoming Busyness

Note: *Holiness involves being set apart and committed to God's purposes, not "checking off" a list of religious to-dos.*

Q-5. Jesus' critics prided themselves in outward religious observances (performance-based religion). What do Jesus' words tell us about the difference between rule-keeping and a right relationship with God (Mark 2:23-27)?

_____

_____

_____

_____

Q-6. How do you understand "The Sabbath was made for man [people]" (Mark 2:27)? What is Jesus really saying here? What does this tell us about resting in God?

_____

_____

_____

_____

Q-7. Jesus is Lord (king) even of the Sabbath (Mark 2:28). How does this impact your thinking and actions about formal worship? About unstructured time with God?

_____

_____

_____

_____

Rest in God's Goodness (Worship)

Q-8. How can you better keep the Sabbath holy without becoming legalistic (like the Pharisees)?

_____

_____

_____

_____

Q-9. Record one important biblical principle (i.e., a promise, command, lesson or truth) you learned from God's word and how you intend to apply it to your life this week. Be specific!

_____

_____

_____

_____

Observation: At its core, the Sabbath is a time to cease (stop) our busyness and "rest" in the goodness of God. It is time spent focusing on who God is, what God has done, and what God is doing and wants to do in our lives!

Key Reminder: "Rest" takes our eyes off of our agenda and focuses them on the one who created, redeemed and restored us, the one who is good!

Lesson 4

Wait Expectantly for God
(Based on Select Psalms)

Personal study: 15 to 20 minutes
Group discussion: 45 to 50 minutes

I s there anyone more beloved in scripture (aside from Jesus) than David, the shepherd boy and king?

David's life was full of action. He served many roles: son; brother; shepherd; warrior; friend; leader. Also, king-in-waiting; man-after-God's-own-heart; song writer; conqueror; celebrity; one beloved of God. Not a bad list!

And yet ... David also knew the hardship of being faithful to God when God seemed "distant." Can you relate?

David experienced the pain of his own sin and that of

those around him. Here, David took on the roles of: fugitive; mourner; adulterer; murderer; rejected husband; hated father; exile, and more.

In both the good and bad of his life, David always (eventually) turned back to God – for direction, forgiveness and hope. He both clung to God and waited on him throughout his life.

Examples of such waiting included:
- While fleeing King Saul's murderous envy and wrath
- While navigating life as king-to-be before actually reigning
- While longing to construct God's temple in Jerusalem and then accepting the reality that God would not let him do so

In all this and more, David rested his life and his future on God's great grace and mercy. His relationship with God was based on God's character, not on David's perfection (or lack thereof). His example is worth emulating.

Now read more about what the Bible says about busyness and waiting expectantly (with faith) for God.

Read Select Psalms

Q-1. What is David doing in these verses (Psalm 5:1-2)? Have you ever done something similar? Explain.

_____

_____

_____

Q-2. What attitude does David connect with waiting (Psalm 5:3; see also Hebrews 11:6)? Why is this attitude important?

_____

_____

_____

Q-3. David tells God's people to include two specific attitudes in their waiting on God (Psalm 27:14). What are these attitudes? How might waiting fortify these traits in our everyday lives?

_____

_____

_____

_____

Note: _Waiting isn't for sissies! It can be emotionally and mentally taxing! And yet, in the midst of busyness, this is often the one "activity" that God calls his children to do!_

Q-4. God's people are called to "wait in hope" (Psalm 33:20 - NIV). Who is the giver of this hope? How do you "wait in hope" in your everyday life?

_____

_____

_____

_____

Q-5. David reminds us that success apart from God is no success at all (Psalm 37:1-2). Have you ever wished for (envied) success that is not aligned with God's word or purposes? Explain.

_____

_____

_____

_____

Q-6. Is David advocating a "name-it-and-claim-it" prosperity theology - that God will always give us our every desire (Psalm 37:3-4)? Why or why not? (Use other scripture to support your answer).

_____

_____

_____

_____

Q-7. What does David counsel in your waiting (Psalm 37:7)? Where have you seen this either in your own life or in the lives of other Christians?

_____

_____

_____

Note: _The Hebrew word transliterated as rest also means to be silent, be still, be mute. ("H1826 - dāmām - Strong's Hebrew Lexicon (KJV)." Blue Letter Bible. Accessed 25 Mar, 2021. https://www.blueletterbible.org//lang/lexicon/lexicon.cfm?Strongs=H1826&t=KJV). It is a time of active listening to and watching for God in our lives._

Q-8. What is the result of waiting "patiently" for the Lord (Psalm 40:1-3)? What impact does your waiting on God have on others (Psalm 40:3)? Where have others seen God at work in your life?

_____

_____

_____

Q-9. While the Psalmist waits, in what does he put his hope (Psalm 130:5-6)? Why does he do this? Why should you?

_____

_____

_____

_____

Q-10. Record one important biblical principle (i.e., a promise, command, lesson or truth) you learned from God's word and how you intend to apply it to your life this week. Be specific!

_____

_____

_____

_____

Observation: Waiting expectantly for God means ... we trust God to do and control what we cannot (or should not) do and control. It is courageous trusting in God's promises and character.

Key Reminder: Waiting on God isn't a sign of weakness; it's an acknowledgement of strength - God's strength!

Lesson 5

Serve Both God and Others
(Based on Luke 10:25-37)

Personal study: 15 to 20 minutes
Group discussion: 45 to 50 minutes

I s it possible to serve others in the midst of our busyness, or do we get a "pass" when life is hectic?

An expert in the religious law approached Jesus and asked what he had to do to inherit eternal life (Luke 10:25-37). Jesus turned the question back to the expert.

The religious leader responded that God's people are to love God with all their being and to love their neighbors as themselves.

Jesus essentially replied, "Right on. Now do it!"

The expert then asked Jesus who his neighbor was. To this, Jesus responded with a story (parable) about a Samaritan (one who was racially mixed, part "Jew," part "pagan," and who melded some Jewish practices with non-scriptural customs). In Jesus' parable, the "hated foreigner" had compassion and mercy on a beaten traveler (while good Jewish leaders walked past).

21

Think, for a moment, about this story from Jesus' listeners' perspective. The Samaritan, an undesirable, social outcast, traveled a road riddled with thieves. He stumbled upon a beaten and robbed traveler, likely a Jew, though Jesus doesn't provide the traveler's ethnic or religious identity. And yet, in compassion, the despised Samaritan surprisingly not only tended to his fellow traveler's immediate needs, he took the traveler to an inn and paid for his ongoing care until the beaten man's health was restored.

Jesus' point is clear: People who do what God desires show mercy to others (even when it disrupts their schedules, even when there's "nothing in it" for them, and even when there may be a cost to their time, reputation or money). Ouch!

The expert in the religious law had posed his question to Jesus to define the limits of his obligation to love others. Jesus' response demonstrated that there are no boundaries in how we are to love others as God himself loves us.

You may be thinking … "Cute story, but … [fill in your personal excuse here]." Jesus' reply to the expert in the law (and to us)? "Go and do likewise."

Now read more about what the Bible says about busyness and serving both God and others.

Read Luke 10:25-37

Q-1. What was the question asked of Jesus by the expert in the law (i.e., the scriptures) (Luke 10:25-26)? Why do you think Jesus turned the question around to have the expert respond?

_____

_____

_____

_____

Q-2. It appears the expert believed his receiving of the inheritance was dependent on <u>his</u> actions and not on the giver of the inheritance. What is typically required of heirs to receive an inheritance? Is the inheritance God provides performance-based (see Eph. 2:8-10)? Explain.

_____

_____

_____

_____

Note: *"Justification is a one-time event (Rom. 3:23-25a), while "sanctification" is God's lifelong training program bringing people into closer alignment with Christ's character (Eph. 4:12-13).*

Q-3. Jesus applauded the expert's response to his question (Luke 10:26-28). How easy is it to love God with the entirety of our being -- heart, soul, strength and mind? How well do you measure up?

_____

_____

_____

_____

Q-4. Why did the religious expert wanted to "justify" himself (Luke 10:29)? Is this something that people still do? Explain.

_____

_____

_____

Q-5. In Jesus' parable, what misfortune fell upon the traveler (Luke 10:30)?

_____

_____

_____

Q-6. Jesus states that a priest and a Levite "passed by on the other side" (Luke 10:31-32). Who were these folks? Why do you think they didn't stop to help?

_____

_____

_____

Q-7. Can you think of a modern-day equivalent to the beaten and robbed traveler? Have you ever failed to respond to another person's pressing needs? If so, describe the situation.

_____

_____

_____

Q-8. What attitude did the Good Samaritan have toward the beaten traveler (Luke 10:33)? How does this reflect God's attitude toward us? Toward the attitude we should have toward others (1 John 3:16-18)?

_____

_____

_____

Serve Both God and Others

Q-9. What word does the expert in the law use to describe the actions of the Good Samaritan toward the beaten traveler (Luke 10:37)? How has God expressed this gift toward you?

_____

_____

_____

_____

Q-10. Are you more likely to show mercy to others when it is convenient or when it is costly? How do you most often express mercy when you are busy?

_____

_____

_____

_____

Q-11. Record one important biblical principle (i.e., a promise, command, lesson or truth) you learned from God's word and how you intend to apply it to your life this week. Be specific!

_____

_____

_____

_____

Overcoming Busyness

Observation: Service may appear to be just one more form of busyness. In fact, it isn't. Busyness most often anchors on "me" and "my agenda." Service tends to anchor on others' needs. Jesus lauded the good Samaritan for selflessly extending God's care to others.

Key Reminder: We are never more like Jesus than when we give ourselves in service to God and others.

Lesson 6

Tend to God's Priorities
(Based on Haggai 1:1-15)

Personal study: 15 to 20 minutes
Group discussion: 45 to 50 minutes

E ver been involved in an effort that seemed to turn to dust before your very eyes? The people of Jerusalem, having returned from exile in Babylon, did!

Through his prophet, Haggai, God told Zerubbabel and Joshua that the people's efforts were futile because they had focused on the wrong priority, not a bad one ... just the wrong one!

In essence, while the people had been busy building "paneled houses" for themselves--think comfortable, cushy homes--they had ignored the task of rebuilding God's temple, the center of their life as God's people and of their worship of God. Oops!

What seemed reasonable and practical to the returning people--a tiny oversight at worst--was no small matter to God.

The result? God saw fit to diminish their harvest, reduce their food stocks, increase their thirst, leave them with "not warm" clothing, and cause them to lose their wages.

Their high expectations in returning to the sweet land God had given their ancestors and had now re-given to them were not met. "What you brought home," said God, "I blew away."

Clearly, the fault was not God's!

God acted in love to draw his wayward children back to him and his priorities through the futility of their efforts - their misguided busyness.

Fortunately, Zerubbabel, Joshua and the whole remnant of people obeyed the voice of the Lord (Haggai 1:12). They repented and moved from "me-focused" busyness to honoring God. As a result, their futility ended.

Please know that not every instance of futility (or calamity) is the result of ungodly priorities. At times, challenges may arise BECAUSE of our obedience to God. Still, God may choose to bring futility into our lives when our busyness does not align with his purposes.

We, too, need to be reminded that God wants our hearts most of all. When our priorities don't align with God's priorities ... futility may result. Failure just may be the loving arms of God directing us back to him!

Now read more about what the Bible says about busyness and tending to God's priorities.

Read Haggai 1:1-15

Tend to God's Priorities

Q-1. What difference does it make that Haggai was conveying God's message--not Haggai's opinions--to Zerubbabel and Joshua (Haggai 1:1-2)? Which holds more weight in your decision-making - God's word or your opinion? Explain.

_____

_____

_____

_____

Q-2. What question does God pose through Haggai (Haggai 1:3-4)? Are "paneled houses" a bad thing? A good thing? Explain. Describe the equivalent of a "paneled house" in your life (something you are striving diligently to obtain or achieve)?

_____

_____

_____

_____

Q-3. God tells Zerubbabel and Joshua to "give careful thought to your ways," (Haggai 1:5,7). Why does God repeat himself? When--if at all--was the last time you paused to view your thoughts, actions, habits--those things that consume your time--in light of God's word?

_____

_____

_____

_____

Q-4. Haggai 1:6 appears to describe an exercise in futility (few results; few achievements; little headway). Is struggle, pain or lack of success ALWAYS a consequence of personal disobedience or punishment? (Read 2 Corinthians 11:24-28, 12:10). Explain.

_____

_____

_____

_____

Q-5. What happened to the people's hard work and expectations (Haggai 1:8-11)? Have you experienced something similar? In retrospect, did your futility draw you closer to God? If so, how?

_____

_____

_____

_____

Q-6. Haggai 1:12 tells us that Zerubbabel, Joshua and the whole remnant of the people obeyed God and Haggai's message. In what area is God calling you to obey and fear him today?

_____

_____

_____

_____

Tend to God's Priorities

Note: *The Hebrew word transliterated as "fear" (vs. 12) can also mean to stand in awe, to inspire reverence, and to honor or respect*

Q-7. What was God's healing message to the people (Haggai 1:13)? Is this same statement true for us? (See Deuteronomy 31:8; Matthew 28:20.) If so … what difference does this make in your everyday life?

_____

_____

_____

_____

Q-8. Read Haggai 1:14-15. Who "stirs up our spirit" (i.e., moves our hearts) to accomplish God's purposes? What difference does it make in the effectiveness of our witness and ministry?

_____

_____

_____

Q-9. Record one important biblical principle (i.e., a promise, command, lesson or truth) you learned from God's word and how you intend to apply it to your life this week. Be specific!

_____

_____

_____

_____

Overcoming Busyness

Observation: Futility results from doing "our thing" our way (John 15:1-8).

Key Reminder: God desires more for us than our comfort, achievement, and success; he desires our hearts in alignment with his will.

Lesson 7

Be Rich Toward God
(Based on Luke 12:13-21)

Personal study: 15 to 20 minutes
Group discussion: 45 to 50 minutes

S uccess! It turns out the "American Dream" isn't so American after all. Success is a universal longing. Work hard. Compete. Win. Relax!

Jesus spoke to this desire when a man asked Jesus to get involved in a dispute he had with his brother about the family inheritance (Luke 12:13-21).

Jesus' words to the brother who wanted "his share?" I'll paraphrase: "Don't be greedy; there's more to life than stuff!"

Success has that effect on us. We become so engaged in this pursuit that we lose sight of what's priceless, real and lasting. We lock in on the temporary instead of the eternal.

To help bring his point home, Jesus shared a parable (story), often referred to as the parable of the rich fool.

Nowhere does Jesus condemn the man for working hard, for good planning or the ability to harvest the bumper crop. Being rich and having possessions isn't the issue.

Instead, Jesus calls the man a fool for selfishly focusing on his wealth instead of his relationship with God. In the parable, the fool purposefully distanced himself from God, and the relationship that God sought to have with him as a dearly loved child.

This is more than an interesting Bible story. It is a strong warning from Jesus that our relationship with the Father must be our primary concern.

Whatever we spend our hours striving for--money, reputation, stuff--is ultimately unsatisfying if we do not embrace the living relationship with God offered through Christ.

Now read more about what the Bible says about busyness and being rich toward God.

Read Luke 12:13-21

Q-1. Why do you think the person in the crowd wanted to get Jesus involved in the dispute he was having with his brother (Luke 12:13)?

_____

_____

_____

_____

Q-2. What does Jesus suggest is the real reason behind the request (Luke 12:14-15)? Why do you think Jesus strips away all pretense from the man's question?

_____

_____

_____

Q-3. Jesus' parable begins by noting "the ground … produced an abundant harvest," (Luke 12:16). Was the man in control of this variable or just benefiting from God's blessings? Explain.

_____

_____

_____

Q-4. How frequently do you pause to give thanks to God for the knowledge, abilities, skills, relationships, etc., that make your accomplishments possible? What does this tell you about taking personal credit for God's gifts?

_____

_____

_____

Q-5. What dilemma did the farmer face (Luke 12:17)? Is there anything wrong with being blessed with abundance? Explain.

_____

_____

_____

Overcoming Busyness

Q-6. What are some modern-day equivalents to "building bigger barns" (Luke 12:18)? What would be a "bigger barn" in the life of your neighbors? In your life?

_____

_____

_____

Q-7. The farmer in Jesus' parable believed he had "made it," that he was successful (Luke 12:19-21). Why, then, does God call him a "fool?"

_____

_____

_____

Q-8. Was the farmer's success rooted in what is temporary or in what is eternal? Explain.

_____

_____

_____

_____

Q-9. What does it mean to be "rich toward God" (Luke 12:21)? Does your busyness promote or detract from being rich toward God? Explain.

_____

_____

_____

Be Rich Toward God

Q-10. Write what you think is God's definition of "success."

_____

_____

_____

_____

Q-11. Record one important biblical principle (i.e., a promise, command, lesson or truth) you learned from God's word and how you intend to apply it to your life this week. Be specific!

_____

_____

_____

_____

Observation: Even our ability to love God (to be "rich toward God") is dependent on God's grace and mercy extended toward us in Christ. We can only love God because he first loved us.

Key Reminder: *"Busyness" without a relationship with God can never lead to true success.*

Lesson 8

Pray for God's Will
(Based on Matthew 26:36-45, 6:7-10)

Personal study: 15 to 20 minutes
Group discussion: 45 to 50 minutes

It was Passover, the time when Jesus would be arrested and crucified to atone for people's sin. It was the evening before Jesus would fulfill the very purpose for which he came to earth.

A million thoughts must have flooded his mind. And yet, on this most important night in human history, Jesus did what he had done countless times before: he retreated to a quiet place to pour out his heart in prayer to his heavenly Father.

In examining Jesus' prayer on Gethsemane, we see both his honest transparency and his perfect submission to his

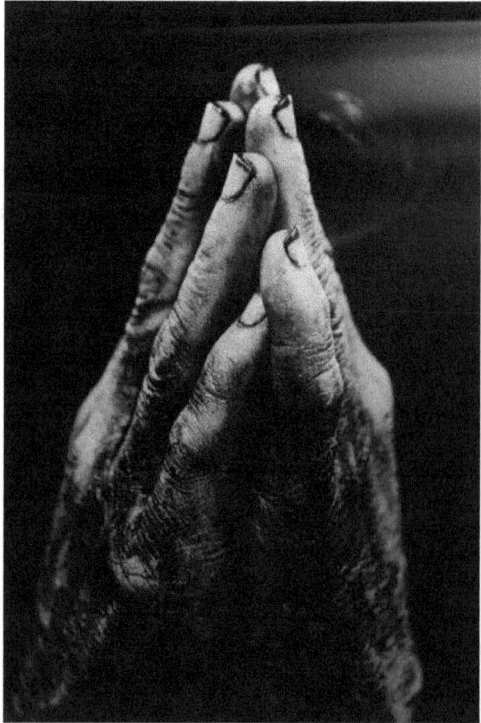

Father. Jesus genuinely brought his deep sorrow to his Father and asked that "this cup" (his crucifixion and death; his separation from the Father; the punishment he would endure in taking all of humanity's sin upon himself) be taken from him. No one would desire to undergo that!

And yet, instead of resting (sleeping) to gain physical reserves for the ordeal ahead, Jesus took time to pray and to submit his will to the Father.

What does Jesus' prayer have to do with busyness of our lives? In fact, quite a bit!

Every day we are faced with a similar choice. We can go it alone or … we can seek to listen to God and do his will. The first option costs us little. It follows our natural inclinations ... but is ultimately fruitless. The second option requires that we humbly submit our desires to God's purposes. Only this choice, however, produces lasting impact, empowering us to accomplish what God himself desires.

Too busy to pray? We're actually too weak not to!

Now read more about what the Bible says about busyness and praying for God's will.

Read Matthew 26:36-45, 6:7-10

Q-1. Following his last supper with his disciples, Jesus went to the Mount of Olives, to a place called Gethsemane (Matthew 26:30, 36). What did Jesus come to do? Where do you most often meet with God in prayer?

_____

_____

_____

_____

Overcoming Busyness

Q-2. What was Jesus' attitude as he approached Gethsemane (Matthew 26:37-38)? What does this tell you about how and when to approach God? About being honest before God?

_____

_____

_____

Note: The Greek word translated "overwhelmed with sorrow" is a superlative meaning intensely sad, and overcome with sorrow so much as to cause one's death. ("G4036 - perilypos - Strong's Greek Lexicon (KJV)." Blue Letter Bible. Accessed 25 Mar, 2021. https://www.blueletterbible.org//lang/lexicon/lexicon.cfm?Strongs=G4036&t=KJV). This is reflected in Luke's account of Jesus prayer where Jesus' "sweat was like drops of blood" (Luke 22:44).

Q-3. What did Jesus ask of his Father (Matthew 26:39)? Did God respond by giving Jesus what he asked (read Matthew 27:45-50)? Why?

_____

_____

_____

_____

Q-4. What does it mean to submit your desires to God's will (Matthew 26:39)? How does this relate to the things that you most desire, value and in which you invest your time?

_____

_____

_____

Pray for God's Will

Note: *God is big enough to handle our heartfelt negative emotions (e.g., anger, sadness, frustration, fear, disappointment, confusion, embarrassment, impatience and more). Jesus poured out his heart to the Father, asking that God remove the suffering he was about to face. But then, he submitted himself to his Father's purposes. Similarly, we can be sure God hears our prayers, regardless of our emotional state, and God will answer according to his will.*

Q-5. What had Jesus asked of his disciples (Matthew 26:38, 40-41)? Why is it important that people join in shared prayer? Tell of a time when you joined in prayer for and with others.

_____

_____

_____

Q-6. The result of Jesus' obedience to his Father was joy (read Hebrews 12:1-2). What was accomplished through Jesus' obedience? Why is this good news?

_____

_____

_____

_____

Q-7. Jesus goes off to pray a second time AND then a third time, largely repeating the same prayer (Matthew 26:42-43). Why persist? Can you trust God to hear you? Why?

_____

_____

_____

Q-8. When Jesus taught his disciples to pray (what we now commonly refer to as "The Lord's Prayer"), he noted that we should ask God to accomplish his will (Matthew 6:7-10). Why is it important for this to be a focus in your prayers?

_____

_____

_____

_____

Q-9. What do you need to change to have your prayers better align with God's will?

_____

_____

_____

Q-10. Record one important biblical principle (i.e., a promise, command, lesson or truth) you learned from God's word and how you intend to apply it to your life this week. Be specific!

_____

_____

_____

Observation: God both hears and answers the prayers of his children. We may not receive that which we desire, but we will <u>always</u> receive that which God deems best for us!

Key Reminder: *We may FEEL too busy to pray, but we are too weak not to!*

Lesson 9

Allow for Holy Interruptions
(Based on Matthew 15:21-28,
Mark 7:24-30)

Personal study: 15 to 20 minutes
Group discussion: 45 to 50 minutes

We've all been there: A day full of people, activity, work and more. We're tired, emotionally drained and longing for some rest and relaxation.

At just this moment, someone (or something) interrupts, and the quiet we longed for is gone.

Jesus had such an experience (Matthew 15:21-28 and Mark 7:24-30). Just prior to this interruption, Jesus had been spiritually jousting with Pharisees and teachers of the law about "being clean" before God.

These critics wanted nothing more than to prove their spiritual superiority (for what it's worth … they failed!).

The Bible states that Jesus then withdrew to the region of Tyre and Sidon (modern-day Lebanon). Jesus wanted some time

away from the throng. So, he chose a placed that was filled with Gentiles (non-Jews; people the Jews considered "outside" of God's family").

It was here that a Canaanite woman interrupted Jesus with an urgent, personal request: "Heal my daughter."

In Jewish thinking, to be both a Gentile AND a woman meant that this mom had little (no) standing to ask for anything. And yet … Jesus does not reject her for interrupting his rest, but complies with her request. This highlights that all who come to him in faith are included in God's family. Jesus set aside "me time" to serve a greater purpose.

Similarly, an interruption in the midst of our busy lives may serve a holy purpose – if we allow it. Do we?

Now read more about what the Bible says about busyness and interruptions in our lives.

Read Matthew 15:21-28, Mark 7:24-30

Q-1. Why is it significant that Jesus sought rest in the Gentile (non-Jewish) city of Tyre (Matthew 15:21-22; Mark 7:24)? What does the woman's use of the term "Son of David" tell us about her knowledge of Jesus and/or his reputation?

_____

_____

_____

_____

Q-2. What is the woman's request of Jesus (Matthew 15:22 and Mark 7:25-26)? On whose behalf was she pleading for compassion?

_____

_____

_____

_____

Q-3. Is it appropriate to desperately called out to Jesus with our or another's needs? Why? If you have done so, what was the situation?

_____

_____

_____

_____

Note: Jesus never said, "Stop bugging me; I'm too busy." Both his silence AND his words eventually drew out the woman's response of faith.

Q-4. Jesus was silent, and his disciples simply wanted to give the woman the brush off (Matthew 15:23). When are you most likely to ignore someone's need? Why?

_____

_____

_____

_____

Q-5. Jesus next basically says, "Sorry, you don't belong to the right group," (Matthew 15:24-25). What was the purpose of Jesus' reply? How did the mother respond (Matthew 15:25)? How do you respond when you receive an initial "no" from God?

_____

_____

_____

_____

Note: The Hebrew word translated "Lord" (vs. 25) means one to whom a person or thing belongs, the possessor or disposer of a thing; a title showing respect and reverence as a servant to one's master ("G2962 - kyrios - Strong's Greek Lexicon (KJV)." Blue Letter Bible. Accessed 30 Mar, 2021. https://www.blueletterbible.org//lang/lexicon/lexicon.cfm?Strongs=G2 962&t=KJV).

Q-6. When praying, how do you distinguish between God's "no, never," and God's "no, not yet?" Respond from your own perspective or experience.

_____

_____

_____

_____

Q-7. Once again, Jesus gives the woman a discouraging reply (Matthew 15:26-27 & Mark 7:27-28). What does the woman's reference to "crumbs" convey? In what area/s do you most need to persist in prayer?

_____

_____

_____

_____

Q-8. Jesus then acknowledges the woman's great faith and heals her daughter (Matthew 15:28 and Mark 7:29-30). What does this passage teach about the importance of people versus the importance of schedules? About God's desire that you persistently call out to him?

_____

_____

_____

_____

Q-9. Record one important biblical principle (i.e., a promise, command, lesson or truth) you learned from God's word and how you intend to apply it to your life this week. Be specific!

_____

_____

_____

_____

Overcoming Busyness

Observation: Jesus commended the Canaanite woman for her faith, despite his apparent, initial "rejection" of her requests. Jesus allowed himself to be interrupted so that the Father's love could flow to a mother in need.

Key Reminder: God is never too busy to care for his children, and we should follow his lead.

Lesson 10

Receive and Share Jesus' Welcome

(Based on Mark 9:33-37, Matthew 25:31-40)

Personal study: 15 to 20 minutes
Group discussion: 45 to 50 minutes

How are busy people supposed to treat one another? More personally, how do you like to be treated?

Jesus' disciples got into a tussle over greatness, specifically THEIR greatness (Mark 9:33-37). They believed, wrongly, that if Jesus chose one of them as his "number two guy," that person would wield greater authority, power, influence and control above others in Jesus' kingdom.

Jesus, however, didn't measure greatness by this standard. In fact, he picked up a little child and said, "welcome the likes of this tyke and you've mastered greatness!" That was unexpected news to Jesus' disciples.

Why did Jesus make this outrageous statement? What is it about "welcoming children" that wins the day? After all, children are not powerful or influential. In fact, they are often the opposite of those traits!

Jesus' words are no less true today than they were 2,000+ years ago. Seeking greatness? Try "welcome" in the name of Christ! Seeking relief from busyness? Receive Jesus' loving welcome!

Unfortunately, finding time for others in our busy lives is a challenge. And yet … welcome reflects God's heart toward all people - especially those who are neglected, overlooked and powerless. It reflects his heart toward you!

Jesus desires that you both embrace his welcome (grace, mercy, forgiveness) AND pass that same welcome to others.

Now read more about what the Bible says about busyness and receiving Jesus' welcome.

Read Mark 9:33-37, Matthew 25:31-40

Q-1. What did Jesus catch his disciples arguing about on the way to Capernaum (Mark 9:33-34)?

_____

_____

_____

Q-2. Why didn't the disciples respond to Jesus' question (Mark 9:34)? Have you ever been caught in an embarrassing "me-focused" conversation? Describe.

_____

_____

_____

_____

Q-3. What does it mean to be "very last" and "servant of all" (Mark 9:35)? What might that look like in your life today?

_____

_____

_____

_____

Q-4. What does Jesus do with the little child (Mark 9:36)? Why do you think this action was both so visible AND so intimate?

_____

_____

_____

_____

Q-5. What does Jesus instruct the disciples to do (Mark 9:37)? Who are you welcoming when you offer kindness to the hurting and neglected?

_____

_____

_____

_____

Note: _The Greek word used for welcome here means taking by the hand, of favorably receiving, of receiving into one's family, of taking upon one's self ("G1209 - dechomai - Strong's Greek Lexicon (KJV)." Blue Letter Bible. Accessed 25 Mar, 2021. https://www.blueletterbible.org//lang/lexicon/lexicon.cfm?Strongs=G1 209&t=KJV). Welcome is more than social politeness; it is fully embracing and loving the person, even at cost to self._

51

Q-6. Who might be considered "little children" in your sphere of influence?

_____

_____

_____

_____

Q-7. When Jesus returns and gathers all nations before him, he will give his inheritance to his people (Matthew 25:31-34). How does Jesus describe those who will receive God's inheritance (Matthew 25:35-40)?

_____

_____

_____

_____

Q-8. Does your welcome of others reflect God's welcome of you (Matthew 25:40)? How might you be more Christ-like in your welcome of others?

_____

_____

_____

_____

Q-9. Record one important biblical principle (i.e., a promise, command, lesson or truth) you learned from God's word and how you intend to apply it to your life this week. Be specific!

_____

_____

_____

_____

Observation: The act of welcome toward the undeserving (little children) reflects God's very heart.

Key Reminder: Every person has a need to be known and loved (in essence, to be welcomed!). Christians have both the responsibility AND the joy of sharing the message that "God loves you in Christ" - even when we are busy!

Leader Appendix

F or those who are leading or facilitating this *Overcoming Busyness* study within a small group, I've included some brief resources to assist in this task. These include:

- Facilitation Guidelines
- Recommended Timeframe for Group Discussion
- Lesson Overviews

Please recognize that these resources are optional. Please use (or ignore) them as you deem appropriate.

Facilitation Guidelines

Below are some general guidelines for leaders to aid your small group discussions:

1. **Keep the big goal in focus**. The goal of this study is to help participants focus on what God is saying to them through his word. There will inevitably be conversational side trips focused on the opinions of experts, hypothetical situations, and/or unrelated topics. When this occurs, gently redirect your group back to God's word, and always seek to let scripture interpret scripture.

2. **Encourage participation by all.** Some people love to talk. Others prefer remaining silent. Draw out the reluctant by communicating the expectation that everyone will answer at least one or two questions during your time together. As for those who may dominate conversations, arrange a separate

(and private) post-study conversation reminding them of the importance of allowing everyone to share. This may mean asking a talker to identify several questions, in advance, that he or she would like to verbally respond to, but then holding back on other questions to allow others to share.

3. **Be welcoming and encouraging.** There is no more valuable activity than spending time in God's word to better know his character, promises and commands. Warmly welcome each participant, regardless of whether they are a Bible rookie, scholar or skeptic. Also, always be encouraging as wrestling with God's truth can, at times, be uncomfortable.

4. **Model transparency but allow for privacy.** Some of the study questions are deeply personal. "How have you experienced ... ?" "Tell of a time when ... ?" It's likely that not everyone in your group will initially feel comfortable sharing their personal stories. That's okay. Encourage participants to share, but do not demand answers to personal questions. If appropriate, share your personal responses (lead by example).

5. **Start and end on time.** Each week make it your practice to both start and end on time. This is fair and courteous to all. Should the original timeframe you agreed upon as a group no longer work for one or more individuals, consider having a separate group conversation to see if the time you've allotted needs to be revised.

6. **Respect each other's privacy.** Make it known that what's said in the group stays in the group. All conversations that take place within the group should be held in confidence UNLESS the individual specifically gives participants personal permission to share his or her news with others.

7. **Don't be the "answer woman/man."** Your task is to facilitate, NOT to provide the group with "right answers." Seek to surface possible answers by asking additional questions, by encouraging additional responses from other participants, and by always pointing participants back to scripture itself. Also remember that it's okay to leave some issues "open." This may lead to additional conversation and learning in the future.

8. **Watch for nonverbal signals.** At times, group members will convey important messages to you nonverbally. Averted eyes, crossed arms, pressed lips, sullen faces may convey messages of disinterest, boredom, defensiveness, internal struggle, and more. If necessary, help refocus the group by reminding them of your purpose. You might also have private, post-session conversations asking "How are things going?," or "You seemed a bit distracted; is there anything I can do to help you get more from the study?" The goal is to encourage participants in their study of God's word.

9. **Prepare**. Read the lesson (including the Scriptures) and personally answer the questions prior to leading your group in discussion. Ask God to speak to you personally through his word so that you might better know and love him.

10. **Pray.** Though last on this list, this task is the most important thing a facilitator can do. Pray for God's blessing upon each participant. Only God can open eyes. Only God can move hearts. Only God can create faith. Only God can make truth personal and relevant. Ultimately, the success of your group rests NOT in your abilities to facilitate but in God's presence in his word and through his Spirit. Count on him to be with you and to empower you to lead your group effectively.

Recommended Timeframe for Group Discussion (45 to 50 minutes)

- **Settling in (5 minutes).** Greet participants and allow time for them to find their seats. Offer pertinent announcements.

- **Opening prayer (2 minutes).** Thank God for the truth conveyed in his word. Ask him to send his Spirit to be your teacher, and to help each study participant find at least one truth or lesson to "grab hold of" in a practical way in daily life.

- **Study itself (35 minutes).** The opening introduction to the lesson (first page or two) need not be read aloud (most participants will have already read this prior to gathering as a group; some will not have read this intro). Determine in advance if you find it valuable to include this introduction. ALWAYS, however, read aloud the entire biblical text of each lesson before beginning to answer the questions. You can ask for one or more volunteers to read the assigned Bible passage/s. Next, read each lesson question and ask group members to respond and discuss.

- **Closing prayer (3 minutes).** Offer a heartfelt closing prayer, praising God for his sovereignty, thanking him for his truth, inviting him to continue working in the life of each participant, and asking him to bless and protect your group members. Also lift up personal prayer requests if agreed to by group members. If desired, the closing prayer can be rotated among others in the group (but only if others agree, in advance, to do so).

Lesson Overviews

Lesson 1: Focus on God's To-Dos

Life is full of necessary "to-dos." In Jesus' interactions with Mary and Martha (Luke 10:38-42), Jesus makes a distinction between what's important and what's MOST important - one's relationship with him! There will always be "to-dos" that need to get done. In fact, some folks are highly wired (driven) to get those to-dos completed! This is not a bad trait. However, when we allow the demands and responsibilities of life to overshadow the nurturing of our relationship with God ... then our priorities are out of whack. Time spent with Jesus will be blessed, and its benefits will never be removed.

Lesson 2: Seek God When Under Pressure

Busyness--with all its urgencies and pressures--often tempts us to to take action WITHOUT God. In part, this is because we, like King Saul, are bad at waiting on God (and seeking his presence and wisdom). King Saul perfectly illustrates someone who attempts to obtain God's blessing through human means (offering animal sacrifices that God's prophet, Samuel, told Saul he [Samuel] would do for Israel). Saul's actions showed disobedience to God's word and God's prophet. Saul simply chose to act based on the pressure of his circumstances. God calls us to greater trust in, and dependence on, him during times of pressure.

Lesson 3: Rest in God's Goodness

God knows we need rest. Physical rest. Emotional rest. Spiritual rest. God specifically calls us to set aside time each week (the Sabbath) to "rest" in God's presence, to remember who God is, what God has done and is doing in our lives. It is a time to recall God's goodness and promises, to worship him, and gather with others for encouragement, fellowship and yes, service to others. This is more than a "checking off a to-do list." It is a time to grow deeper in our understanding of our identity as God's loved, redeemed and forgiven children!

Lesson 4: Wait Expectantly for God

"Waiting on God" is more than ordinary "waiting." It is a reasoned, intentional decision to be dependent on God, a refusal to move forward "unless you [God] go with us," (Exodus 33:15-17)! This waiting is to be done with courage, with heart, and with complete trust in God (which removes all impatience and worry). Believers can wait expectantly on God because his word and promises are forever true. We can wait on God when we are confronted by busyness because he is faithful and loving, and his character never changes.

Lesson 5: Serve Both God and Others

Faith is always made evident through actions. When an expert in the law questioned Jesus about what he--the expert--must do to inherit eternal life, Jesus turns the question back to the man, asking him about his understanding of the scriptures. The expert accurately cites Deuteronomy 6:5 and Leviticus 19:18, ("Love the Lord your God with all your heart and with all your soul and with all your strength and with all your mind;" and, "Love your neighbor as yourself,"). The challenge for the expert, and for us, is less about "the knowing" of the Law than it is "the doing" of it. In asking, "Who is my neighbor?," the expert is acknowledging that he failed this twofold command. The parable of the Good Samaritan demonstrates that busyness is no excuse for obedience; we are to love others, even when there is nothing "in it" for us, and even when that love is "costly." Service is one means of extending God's love to others, even in our busyness.

Lesson 6: Tend to God's Priorities

Despite our best efforts, at times we fail - miserably! Often, there may be no logical explanation for this, simply the brokenness we find in the world. At other times, however, failure and futility are the consequences of personal or collective sin. Haggai told Zerubbabel and Joshua that the people's efforts to rebuild Jerusalem after their return from exile was doomed to futility. This failure was due to the people's neglect of first rebuilding God's temple. Haggai was not just offering his opinion; he was giving God's words to the people. Haggai tells the people (twice) to give careful thought to their ways. In short, he tells them that their actions are not in alignment with God's will. The people's disobedience had led to futility in their other endeavors. In hearing God's word, the people turned from their priorities to God's priorities. God then told the people that he was with them, and the people began working on rebuilding the Lord's temple. God desires that our hearts be in alignment with his will, even in our busyness!

Lesson 7: Be Rich Toward God

The world defines success very differently than God does. God's definition of success has little to do with wealth, though even wealth is a gift from God. The danger lurks in giving our hearts over to those things that only temporarily satisfy - money, reputation, relationships, achievements, etc. Jesus' parable about the rich fool (Luke 12:13-21) reminds us that we are only rich when we have a loving relationship with God. All else will pass into nothingness. Any investment (busyness) that excludes God runs the danger of costing us our very souls.

Lesson 8: Pray for God's Will

God calls us--especially in our busyness--to reach out to him in prayer. This is because our desires must be subordinate to his will. God desires that we reach out to him with the whole of our emotions. God may not give us what we desire, but he hears our prayers and certainly gives us what we need in every situation. Jesus invites us to be persistent in our prayers. We can trust God to know what is best for his glory and for our good. God hears our prayers and knows our needs. We can readily accept his best in answering our prayers, even if that answer is "no."

Lesson 9: Allow for Holy Interruptions

Divine appointments are often found in interruptions to our planned schedules. The Canaanite woman's recognition of Jesus as the "Son of David," indicated that she, more than the Jewish religious leaders, was aware that Jesus was the promised Messiah come to Earth. At times, God's initial "noes" to our requests are simply intended to drive us deeper into pleas for his grace. At others, God's "noes" are intended to help us recognize his sufficiency even in the absence of that which we seek. God prioritizes people over schedules (and so should we!). God is never too busy to care for his children, and we should follow his lead!

Lesson 10: Embody Jesus' Welcome

Busyness often keeps us focused on our agenda (doing, achieving, grasping). In contrast, Jesus calls us to focus on others - especially others who bring nothing to our me-first agendas! Jesus overheard his disciples arguing about greatest, so he told them that greatness is never more evident than when they take the role of a servant, lovingly welcoming those without power or position (like children!). In fact, he tells them that when they welcome little children in his name, they are showing welcome to God the Father! Tending to the needs of the hungry, the thirsty, the naked, the sick, the lonely, prisoners ... is like serving God himself! Our busyness must take a back seat to graciously welcoming (and extending kindness to) others.

Bible Studies by the Author

How God Defines Success

HOW GOD DEFINES SUCCESS

LESSONS IN LIVING A GOD-PLEASING LIFE

Most everyone wants to be successful, but what does "success" really mean for a follower of Christ? Most importantly, how does God describe the life he desires for his people?

How God Defines Success is a 10-lesson Bible study examining how God would have his followers live. It highlights 10 traits that God identifies with true success, such as living for his glory, seeking his guidance, submitting to his will, remaining attached to him, and more!

Success is not something <u>we</u> achieve, but rather, it is something that <u>God</u> provides as we trust and obey him.

A 10-LESSON BIBLE STUDY
DAVID RUSTAD

Conquering Worry and Fear

CONQUERING WORRY AND FEAR

GOD'S ANSWER TO WORRY IS GOD HIMSELF

Many people struggle with worry, yet God does not desire that his children live in a state of fear and apprehension. In fact, he clearly tells us "do not worry," and "do not be afraid." But how?

A 10-LESSON BIBLE STUDY
DAVID RUSTAD

Conquering Worry and Fear is a 10-lesson Bible study exploring how God would have us address worry and grow our trust in him. It offers 10 ways to better lean into God during life's challenges, such as resting in his intimacy, rejoicing in his goodness, focusing on his provision, claiming his sufficiency, and more!

God walks with us in all circumstances, even the nasty ones! God himself is the answer to our worry and fear.

Overcoming Busyness

OVERCOMING BUSYNESS

RESTING IN GOD DURING LIFE'S DEMANDS AND RESPONSIBILITIES

Feel overwhelmed by life's daily responsibilities? Is your life controlled by too many to-dos?

A 10-LESSON BIBLE STUDY
DAVID RUSTAD

Overcoming Busyness is a 10-lesson Bible study examining how God would have us find our strength and rest in him. It highlights 10 ways we can flourish during life's demands and responsibilities, such as receiving and sharing Jesus' welcome, resting in God's goodness (worship), praying for God's will, allowing for holy interruptions, and more!

Whatever the pace (or season) of life, God calls us to give him our busyness so that we can receive the refreshment only he can provide.

About the Author

David Rustad is a communications professional, author and church entrepreneur. He is a follower of Christ who happens to be a lifelong student of the Bible.

Rustad worked in corporate communications, church relations and business development for a Twin Cities-based not-for-profit organization for more than 35 years. He then launched a church survey business to help church leaders better understand the real-life challenges of those they serve.

Through his work surveying church attenders, Rustad found that worry, busyness and misguided notions of success are common challenges in the lives of many. He subsequently developed three Bible studies aimed at helping Christians and non-Christians alike recognize that freedom from worry, busyness and misguided striving only comes through trusting in what God in Christ has done and is doing in their lives.

Rustad is active in lay ministry and cares deeply about the spiritual health and growth of God's people. A Minnesota native, he resides in Saint Paul, Minn., with his wife, Lynne.

Afterword

The older I become the more convinced I am that God's love for me does not depend upon either my spotty performance or the circumstances I find myself facing; it relies on God's unchanging and unfailing character and promises! This means I have peace in what God has done for me in Christ and continues working in me through his Spirit.

I do not know the circumstances of your life. I do not know the number or depth of your daily activities and responsibilities. Perhaps you feel overwhelmed by their near constant demands on your life. I offer this simple advice: give your busyness to God. He is with you (even now), and he is for you!

God will prove himself sufficient in this moment. Lean in. Hold tight. Ask him to direct you in the way forward.

The one who loved you enough to take your sin upon himself on the cross passionately cares for you. Find your strength, your peace, and your rest in him! -- Dave

Acknowledgments

First, "thank you" to the many people who have shown me the beauty of Christ in their words and their actions. The blessing of your presence in my life (and God's presence through you) is more than words can describe. Know that you are a true gift to me, and I thank God for you!

I also offer a special thank you to "the guys" who join me in weekly Bible study: Bill, Andrew, Santiago! Thank you for your willingness to "test drive" this study in its early forms! I am grateful for your feedback and encouragement, and most of all, for your willingness to seek and follow God in your busy lives.

As I've said before, all glory belongs to God alone. Overcoming busyness is allowing God to guide and direct our thinking, actions and lives.

Acknowledgments

Photo Credits

Overcoming Busyness

www.ingramcontent.com/pod-product-compliance
Lightning Source LLC
Chambersburg PA
CBHW060421050426
42449CB00009B/2071